Alad

(an extract)

A pantomime retold by Kaye Umansky

Illustrations by Deborah Jones

Cast

Aladdin
a lazy boy

Widow Twanky
Aladdin's mother

Wishy-Washy
Aladdin's friend

Malafigo
a wicked magician
Ly-Chi
the princess's maid
Princess Tigerlily
the sultan's daughter

Scene One

A busy bazaar

Enter Aladdin, whistling casually. He sneaks an orange from a fruit stall.

Wishy-Washy *(off stage, shouting)* Aladdin!

Enter Wishy-Washy, running, with a heavy bag of washing.

Wishy-Washy *(out of breath)* At last! I've been looking everywhere for you, Aladdin.

Aladdin *(peeling orange)* What's up, Wishy-Washy?

Wishy-Washy You're in trouble. Your mum wants you.

Aladdin Oh, she does, does she?

Wishy-Washy Yes. She said, "Go and find that lazy good-for-nothing, and tell him to come home right now and hang out the washing, or I'll peg him up by his ears!"

Aladdin Why can't **you** do it?

Wishy-Washy You're too heavy! Anyway, I've got to heat the water and fill the tubs before I start on the ironing. Your mum's a slave-driver. It's nothing but work, work, work. Should I hand in my notice, do you think?

Aladdin That's up to you.

Wishy-Washy I can't make decisions. I'm wishy-washy!

Aladdin Well, you know what I always say. Work is fine as long as it doesn't intrude on your spare time.

Wishy-Washy *(gloomily)* I don't get any spare time.

Aladdin You should be like Robinson Crusoe. He had all the work done by Friday!

Wishy-Washy Ha, ha. You won't laugh when your mum catches you. Did you steal that orange?

Aladdin Yep!

Wishy-Washy Well, you shouldn't have. And pick up the peel! It's antisocial to drop litter.

Aladdin So? It's my orange. I can do what I like with it.

Wishy-Washy Well, you'd better eat it quickly, because here comes your mum.

Aladdin Help! I'm hiding.

Aladdin hides behind a barrel.

Widow Twanky *(off stage, shouting)* Alaaadinnnnn!

Enter Widow Twanky with a large basket full of washing. She trips on the orange peel. A huge pair of comedy knickers flies out of the basket.

Widow Twanky Whoopsee! There go the bloomers!

Wishy-Washy *(picking up bloomers)* Hello, Mrs Twanky.

Widow Twanky Oh, there you are, Wishy-Washy. Have you found Aladdin yet?

Wishy-Washy Um, no.

Widow Twanky Fibber! I saw you talking to him. He's hiding around here somewhere, isn't he? I wonder where.

Aladdin bobs up and makes faces behind Widow Twanky's back.

Audience He's behind you!

Aladdin bobs back down as Widow Twanky looks behind her.

Widow Twanky Where?

Widow Twanky looks forward again and Aladdin bobs up.

Audience Behind you!

Aladdin bobs back down again as Widow Twanky looks behind her.

Widow Twanky Where? I can't see him.

Wishy-Washy That's because your glasses are steamed up.

Widow Twanky You're right. My wipers have jammed! *(Takes glasses off and polishes them)* **I'm** steamed up, not just my glasses. That lazy boy!

Wishy-Washy Oh, he's not so bad. At least he brightens up the place.

Widow Twanky Yes, because he never turns the lights off! Oh, well. When you see him, tell him to get back home, or I'll put him through the mangle!

Exit Widow Twanky. Aladdin comes out from behind the barrel.

Aladdin Thanks, Wishy-Washy. You're a good friend. Here, have the orange. *(Hands Wishy-Washy orange)* If your conscience will let you.

Wishy-Washy Cor! Thanks. *(hesitates)* Should I? *(to audience)* Would you?

Audience Yes! No!

Wishy-Washy Oh, go on then! *(takes orange)*

Aladdin Someone's coming. It's not Mum again, is it?

Aladdin and Wishy-Washy retreat to a quieter corner of the bazaar. Enter Princess Tigerlily and Ly-Chi, disguised with long cloaks.

Ly-Chi My lady! Shouldn't we be getting back to the palace? You're dining with your father at eight.

Princess Tigerlily Oh, but Ly-Chi! I want to visit the bazaar. Please! Just a bit longer.

Ly-Chi You know how cross he gets when you're late.

Princess Tigerlily I don't care. He'll only drone on about husbands again.

Ly-Chi You'll have to get married one day.

Princess Tigerlily I don't see why, if I don't meet anybody I like. Father thinks money's everything, but I don't. If I marry at all, he's got to be … I don't know … friendly, and funny.

Ly-Chi Kind.

Princess Tigerlily Generous.

Ly-Chi And brave.

Princess Tigerlily All those things. Rich would be nice, because that would keep Father happy. But poor is fine too.

Ly-Chi Sultans' daughters don't marry commoners.

Princess Tigerlily Well, we'll see, won't we? Oh, look! Fresh figs! Let's get some.

Princess Tigerlily and Ly-Chi walk among the stalls. Aladdin and Wishy-Washy look on.

Aladdin *(excitedly)* Did you hear that? It's her!

Wishy-Washy Who?

Aladdin Her! Princess Tigerlily. The sultan's daughter, you idiot!

Wishy-Washy Really? She doesn't look much like a princess.

Aladdin That's because she's in disguise. Don't you ever wash your ears out?

Wishy-Washy Only on Sundays. I'm too busy washing laundry the rest of the time, aren't I? Come on, let's go. You've got to face the music some time.

Aladdin You go. I'll be there soon.

Wishy-Washy Aw, Aladdin ...

Aladdin Oh, and let's have the orange back.

Wishy-Washy But you said ...

Aladdin Come on, give!

Wishy-Washy shrugs, throws Aladdin the orange and exits.

Aladdin *(to audience)* Right! Here goes.

Aladdin steps into the path of Princess Tigerlily and Ly-Chi, who are about to leave the bazaar.

Aladdin *(bowing)* Ladies! I couldn't help overhearing what you were saying.

Princess Tigerlily Do you always eavesdrop on private conversations?

Aladdin Only the good parts! Like the bit where you said you like people to be *friendly*, *funny*, *kind*, *generous* and *brave*. I'm all of those. And handsome too!

Ly-Chi And modest, no doubt.

Aladdin Absolutely! Right, I've done **friendly,** now I'm moving on to **funny.** Have you heard the one about the frog, the chopsticks, and the bowl of rice? There was this frog and …

Princess Tigerlily Stop right there. I've heard it.

Ly-Chi *(to Aladdin)* You really must excuse us. *(To Princess Tigerlily)* Come on, my lady.

Aladdin *(aside) Friendly, funny … kind. (To Princess Tigerlily)* I say! Don't you just love fluffy little kittens?

Ly-Chi He's mad! Let's go.

Aladdin *(desperate to impress)* Here! Have an orange. *(Thrusts orange into Princess's hand)* See how **generous** I am?

Princess Tigerlily and Ly-Chi start to walk away.

Aladdin Hey! I think I'll just go and pick a fight with someone bigger than me, because I'm soooo **brave** …

Princess Tigerlily *(giggling)* He's funny.

Ly-Chi He's crazy! Come on.

Exit Princess Tigerlily and Ly-Chi.

Aladdin *(shouting)* I live in the first alley on the right. The wash-house! Twanky Washing Inc. We do a special offer on disguises! *(To himself)* Oh, rats! I've blown it.

Aladdin sinks down in despair. The stage darkens. Thunder rumbles. Enter Malafigo, in a dark corner.

Malafigo *(in an evil voice)* Ha, ha, ha, ha!

Audience Sssss!

Malafigo *(to audience)* Oh, yes, you're brave now, aren't you? While you're in a gang. But you wouldn't dare on your own! You'd better show some respect, or I won't tell you my evil plan.

Audience Boooo!

Malafigo *(to audience)* Oh, all right. I'll tell you anyway, so you know who you're dealing with! I am the mighty magician, Malafigo, and right now I'm looking for a boy. A nimble boy. A boy with no particular purpose in life. Preferably a stupid boy whom I can bend to my will. A boy like … *(Spots Aladdin)* … that boy!

Audience Booo!

Malafigo *(to audience)* Oh, shut up! I can't be bothered with you anymore. I've got other fish to fry.

Malafigo approaches Aladdin.

Malafigo Ho there, lad!

Aladdin *(standing up)* Oh, hello.

Malafigo You know, I'm almost sure I know you from somewhere. What's your name?

Aladdin Aladdin.

Malafigo What? Such a coincidence! Can it be?

Aladdin *(puzzled)* What?

Malafigo Aladdin, son of … ?

Aladdin Abu the tailor.

Malafigo *(excitedly)* It is! Tell me, boy. Your dear father. Is he well?

Aladdin Not really. He died years ago, when I was a baby. There's only Mum and me.

Malafigo Oh, no! My poor brother!

Aladdin *(surprised)* Brother?

Malafigo Yes, nephew. I am Malafigo, your poor father's brother. I have been away these long years. I had not heard the tragic news.

Aladdin I never knew Dad had a brother.

Malafigo Sadly, we parted on bad terms. But now I'm back and ready to make amends to his widow and his fine son. Come, Aladdin. Lead me to your poor mother.
(Aside) Perfect! Ha, ha, ha!

Exit Aladdin and Malafigo.

Scene Two

Inside Twanky Washing Inc

Widow Twanky is scrubbing items of comedy clothing in a foaming tub. Wishy-Washy is slumped over the ironing board, snoring.

Wishy-Washy	Zzzzzzzz!
Widow Twanky	*(throwing a bar of soap at Wishy-Washy)* Wake up, Wishy-Washy! You're not paid to sleep.
Wishy-Washy	*(suddenly awake)* Ow! That hurt! *(Rubs head)* I was having a lovely dream, too.
Widow Twanky	What about?
Wishy-Washy	You doubled my wages.
Widow Twanky	Well, you can spend them in your next dream. Where is that boy, Aladdin? Just wait till he gets home …

Wishy-Washy starts the ironing. Enter Aladdin and Malafigo.

Wishy-Washy Uh-oh.

Widow Twanky *(crossly)* Where have you been, Aladdin? Here I am, working my fingers to the bone and … Ooh, who's this?

Aladdin Mum, meet Uncle Malafigo – Dad's brother. We just met by chance in the bazaar and …

Widow Twanky Brother? Your father didn't have a brother.

Malafigo Ah. You're wrong there, good woman.

Aladdin He says they parted on bad terms.

Malafigo We did. Oh, woe, woe, we did. I always intended to look him up, and now it's too late. Boo hoo!

Malafigo weeps on Widow Twanky's shoulder.

Wishy-Washy Oh, dear! *(Takes out comedy hanky and blows nose loudly)* He's started me off now.

Widow Twanky *(softly)* There, there. Cheer up. It was a long time ago.

Malafigo Oh, boo, hoo, hoo! Abu! Abu! You're dead, it's true! What can I do?

Widow Twanky I wouldn't try writing poetry.

Malafigo Tell me, poor woman. How can I honour Abu's memory and help you and your poor child?

Widow Twanky Well, since you ask, I could do with one of those newfangled washing machines.

Malafigo A washing machine? Madam, I will buy you an entire launderette! Wall to wall twin tubs. Imagine!

Widow Twanky Can I have one of those fancy wall-mounted soap dispensers?

Malafigo Of course.

Wishy-Washy What about a new iron?

Malafigo Anything! My purse is at your disposal. *(Takes out purse)* Here, take it! Spend it all!

Widow Twanky Oh, I couldn't possibly.

Malafigo But I insist.

Widow Twanky Well, in that case … *(Snatches purse and stuffs it down her dress)*

Malafigo And that's just the beginning. I want to do something for this splendid lad of yours.

Widow Twanky Splendid? What ... Aladdin?

Malafigo Such a fine boy. You must be very proud.

Widow Twanky Um ... well, I might be if I ever saw him. His life's one long lunch break.

Malafigo You see? Clearly destined to be a business executive. Nephew, I'm going to take you under my wing. What would you say to a fine carpet shop of your own ... in the smarter part of town?

Aladdin I'd say, thanks very much! As long as it's not too much like hard work.

Malafigo Oh, no. You can employ staff to do everything, and just lie around sipping sherbet!

Aladdin Great! Who will I get for staff, though?

Wishy-Washy Don't look at me. I'll be in the launderette, fixing the vandalised soap dispenser.

Widow Twanky Malafigo, why don't you come into the parlour and have a nice cup of tea. We've got lots to talk about. Aladdin, show our guest through.

Wishy-Washy Can **I** have a cup of tea?

Widow Twanky Certainly not! He's not **your** relative. You stay here and get on with the ironing.

Exit Aladdin, Widow Twanky and Malafigo.

Wishy-Washy Typical! I'm left to do all the work as usual.

Wishy-Washy suddenly snatches up the garment he has been ironing. It has a huge hole burnt in it.

Wishy-Washy Oh, blast!

There is a tap at the door.

Wishy-Washy Come in, it's open.

Enter Ly-Chi.

Ly-Chi Excuse me, is this Twanky Washing Inc?

Wishy-Washy Ink, wine, grass stains, we get them all out – eventually. Can I help you?

Ly-Chi Does a boy live here? Dark hair. Tells jokes.

Wishy-Washy You must mean Aladdin. He's a bit of a joker.

Ly-Chi My mistress is outside. She'd like to speak to him – in private.

Wishy-Washy Ah, yes. The sultan's daughter.

Ly-Chi Sssh! Keep your voice down.

Wishy-Washy Sorry. *(In a deep voice)* Is this down far enough?

Ly-Chi giggles. Enter Aladdin.

Wishy-Washy Aladdin, I thought you were busy sucking up to your new uncle.

Aladdin Mum sent me to buy a welcome-home cake. *(To Ly-Chi)* What brings you here?

Ly-Chi The princess wants a word with you.

Aladdin *(excitedly)* She does? Where is she?

Ly-Chi Waiting outside in the alley. Be quick! We're ever so late.

Exit Aladdin, running.

Scene Three

In the alley, outside Twanky Washing Inc

Princess Tigerlily is waiting outside the wash-house. Enter Aladdin.

Aladdin Princess, you wanted to see me?

Princess Tigerlily Yes. I wanted to thank you for the orange.

Aladdin You're welcome. Shall I tell you the one about the dragon and the one-eyed duck?

Princess Tigerlily *(smiling)* I don't think there's time right now. You're Aladdin, right?

Aladdin How do you know that?

Princess Tigerlily We made enquiries. Listen, Aladdin. I have to get back to the palace. I just wanted to say –

Aladdin What?

Princess Tigerlily Thanks for making me laugh.

Aladdin *(rather disappointed)* That's it?

Princess Tigerlily Yes.

Enter Ly-Chi and Wishy-Washy.

Ly-Chi My lady, we really must go. The sultan …

Princess Tigerlily I know. Goodbye, Aladdin.

Princess Tigerlily and Ly-Chi begin to walk away.

Aladdin Princess?

Princess Tigerlily Yes?

Aladdin I'm going to be rich, too. As well as all the other stuff.

Princess Tigerlily You are? Well, I'm very glad to hear it.

Exit Princess Tigerlily and Ly-Chi.

Wishy-Washy I just hope you know what you're doing, Aladdin.

READY, STEADY, ACT!

This play is a pantomime and it contains lots of comedy and silly jokes.

WHAT YOU WILL NEED

Costumes

- Aladdin and Wishy-Washy – bare feet and bright T-shirts.
- Widow Twanky is the Dame – big dress, wig if possible, silly glasses.
- Tigerlily and Ly-Chi – rich and gorgeous.
- Malafigo – moustache and top hat.

Props

There are lots of props in this play. Make a list; decide what you can find or make. How will you manage the comedy knickers?

Sound and special effects

Could Malafigo come in with a bang?

SPEAKING AND MOVING

When you are performing comedy you have to wait for the audience to finish laughing before you carry on. This is tricky and takes some practice!

Facial expressions are important in pantomime, so pile on the cheekiness, surprise, love, anger. Timing should be just right; practise tripping over the orange peel and flinging the comedy knickers into the air.

> Did you know...?
> In the UK, over ten million people go to a pantomine each year?